Puzzle Pa
Activity Bc

T0044658

Calling all Moshling hunters! Greetings, Buster
Bumblechops, super Moshling expert, here. Now,
although I am fangtastic at catching these tricky little
critters, I might just need your help today, because
a few of them are proving more than a bit difficult
to catch. Keep your eyes peeled (not literally!) in the
pages of this book for Blingo, Shambles, and Gracie,
they're teeny-weeny masters of hide-and-seek.
Happy hunting!

Can you also put your paws on the Hairy Green Paw Chair?

Is your monster brain as brilliant as Monstro City's own super brainiac, Tamara Tesla? Grab a pen, Moshi superfans, and pit your wits against 'our lady of the giant petri dish' (that's Tamara, in case you're still warming up your grey matter!), in this truly tricky fact or fib quiz.

1. Diavlos can fly. FACT FIB

2. Roary Scrawl's favourite food is Eye Pie. FACT FIB

3. The DIY Shop has two eyes on top of the sign. FACT FIB

4. Chomper and Stomper graze in a field at the end of Ooh La Lane. FACT FIB

5. Roxy the Precious Prism wears white gloves. FACT FIB

6. Dr. Strangeglove lost one of his hands when a deranged Musky Husky chewed it thinking it was a pile of sausages. FACT FIB

7. Elmore is the smallest monster in Monstro City. FACT FIB

8. Pooky and Snookums are cute little Puppies. FACT FIB

9. Cap'n Buck sails the seas on his ship called the Cloudy Cloak Clipper. FACT FIB

10. Woolly Blue Hoodoos are never seen without their mystical Staffs of Power. FACT FIB

Roxy's Rockin Rox
Picture Patterns

Rox, Rox, Rox! Rox are a monster's best friend! Rox make the Moshi world go round! Oops, sorry, got carried away there! But seriously fellow furballs, you need these sparkling coloured gems of beauty if you want to shop 'til you drop in the streets of Monstro City.

That priceless prism, Roxy, has been buffing up some shiny Rox for you. Zzing! Check out the blinging display here, grab your colouring pens or pencils and help Roxy add the finishing Rox to each shiny row. Remember – no smudges please!

1

2

3

4

5

6

Roary Scrawl's Word Cross

Roary Scrawl is never normally stuck for words, but he's got his eyes all in a twist. Today's edition of his paper is due to the printers in an hour's time and he hasn't worked out the solutions to the puzzle page yet. Quick, grab a pen and paper, power up your brain and get writing words. You need to fill in the missing letters to complete the ten word cross puzzles, before Roary's peeking peepers pop! Unscrabble the shaded letters to reveal the name of the paper that Roary works on.

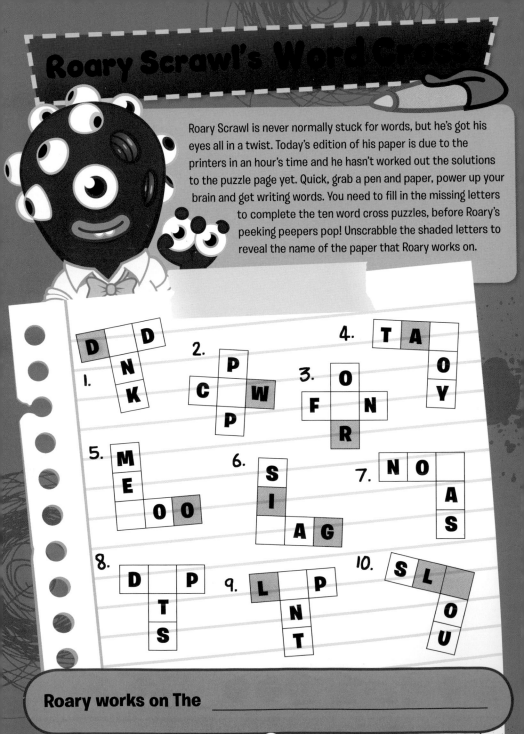

Roary works on The _____

Gilbert Finnster's
Word Shuffle Page

1

Trinkets and Moshling memorabilia are in stock,
sold by the coolest fish on the block.
Do you know the name of this shop?
Think hairy monster, and the penny might drop!
Unshuffle the letters below to find out,
and then give a BIG monster shout!

C	A	P	L	A	S	N	W	S	W

P	g	w	S	N	C	l	a	w	s

2

Gilbert loves Moshlings. Even as a tiny tadpole he monitored his Moshling garden daily in his quest to find out all the seed codes. His Moshling Zoo is pretty full, but he is constantly on the look out for new and rare little critters. Unscrabble the letters to reveal the names of five Moshlings that have come into Gilbert's garden.

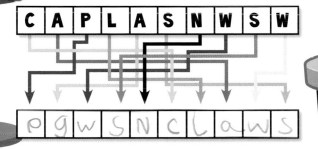

POOHAM

PRIEPPN

GATLINGII

CRVERHMBOB

YER LLO'A

_____

_____

_____

_____

_____

Buster Bumblechops' Mystery Moshlings

Greetings, fellow Moshling hunters! If you go down to the woods today you might just spot some tiny critters. Buster Bumblechops has been trying to track some down but has lost them in the gathering gloom. Look at the shadows and read the clues to help him catch these miniature masters of hide-and-seek. But watch out, you never know who might be lurking amongst the trees!

Wide-eyed 'n bushy-tailed, now you see me, now you don't! Super hero or caped assassin?

Woo-oo-oo! Don't get your plasma in a wobble, or I might just silently turn you inside-out. I'm spooky but not scary.

Zzzzzz! Slumbersome, sleepy and snuffly – ahhhh, yawn, I can hardly keep my eyes open!

Ha, ha, ha, ha! I must text that joke to my fellow funny furball friends. I'm super cute and sensationally stylish!

Master of camouflage? Ferocious and stealthy? Err, I don't think so! More snuggly and cuddly! Please scratch my tummy.

Mizz Snoots' Memory Game

Where do all poshi Moshi Monsters go to shop? Why, Horrods of course! Come and mingle with the mosheratti of Monstro City and meet resident monster beauty Mizz Snoots. Take a good look around the store. Now, turn the page and test your monster memory, to see how poshi a Moshi you really are!

112 Rox

117 Rox

85 Rox

100 Rox

121 Rox

55 Rox

120 Rox

159 Rox

100 Rox

96 Rox

123 Rox

Horrods

Mizz Snoots' Memory Game

Poshi Moshi or Noti?

Top of the posh? Grab a jewel-encrusted pen and practise your prowess. Only truly snooty monsters should take this test!

1. What colour is the bow in Mizz Snoots' hair?

_____

3. How many fish are on the fountain Mizz Snoots is selling on the third shelf?

_____

2. What is peeping out of the big blue vase by the shelves?

_____

4. What is on Mizz Snoots' counter?

_____

5. What colour is the material at the top of the shelves?

_____

6. How many items are on the top shelf?

_____

7. How many Rox is the Lava Lamp?

_____

8. Which directions are the arrows behind Mizz Snoots pointing in?

_____

9. Which delicious Wheelie Yum Yum is whizzing around the shop?

_____

10. What colour is Mizz Snoots dress?

_____

Cap'n Buck's Flag Frenzy

Arrrr! Ahoy me hearties! Cap'n Buck is about to set sail on another salty sea adventure. Study these here ol' flags to see where the intrepid pirate is taking the *Cloudy Cloth Clipper*. Use your noggin' to work out which countries the flags represent. All hands on deck! Are you a land lubber or a true sea dog? Yo, ho, ho . . . you don't want to walk the plank now, do you?

1 ....

2 ....

3 ....

4 ....

5 ....

6 ....

7 ....

8 ....

Shiver me timbers! Now what is this? I don't remember any country having a flag like this.

Design your own flag for an exotic new country that Cap'n Buck can visit. What is your country called?

9

Tamara Tesla's Maths Mash

Tamara has spent another night holed up in her Observatory lab, plotting brain-bashing puzzles and more fiendish monster mental maths tests. Is your buzzing brain up for this tricky challenge? If not, just turn the page and go and clean the furballs out of your ears!

1 0 x 12 = 12

2 77 ÷ 11 =

3 102 - 17 =

4 1 + 2 + 3 + 4 + 5 + 6 =

5 What number comes next in this sequence?

2   4   8   16   32

6 Fill in the missing numbers in this sequence:

11   22   _   44   _   66

7 Put these numbers in the correct order. The digits increase by 6 each time:

31   67   55   85   61   37   79   73   43   49

8 A lump of Green costs 42 Rox. How much will four lumps cost? ___ Rox

9 An Arm Chair originally cost 100 Rox, but you only want to pay 75% of that price. How much will you have to pay? ___ Rox

10 Billy Bob Baitman has caught twenty-seven boots. How many pairs of boots can he make with these. How many will be left over?

11 Moe Yukky took three and a quarter hours to clean up his shop. How many minutes is that? ___ minutes

12 You have 84 Rox. You spend 23 Rox on a Spicy Dragon Roll and 15 Rox on a bowl of Gloop Soup.

How much do you spend? ___ Rox

How many Rox do you have left? ___ Rox

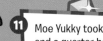
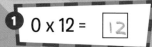

Prof. Purplex's
Bookish Banquet

This purple birdie boffin is brainier than a big brain pie with extra brain sprinkles! Owls of Wiseness don't just scoff encyclopedias though, they'll eat any book they can get their wings on! Design some book covers below for the Prof.'s next bookish banquet.

Tyra Fang's
Colourful Crazy Quilts

Goo York! Goo York! I want to wake up in that Monstro City that never sleeps . . . under a roarsome homemade quilt crafted by my own fair paws!

The Goo York queen of fashion has got her quilts all in a quiver. Tamara Tesla has made seventeen beautiful quilts to display in Tyra's Spa. There are eight pairs of matching quilts, and one unique design. Tyra needs your help to find the odd-quilt-out, as she wants to take it home to hang on her wall. Match the other seven pairs for Tyra's display, before she has a monster model hissy fit!

A   B   C   D   E

F   G   H   I   J

K   L   M   N   O

Ruby Scribblez's
Scare Squares and Blocks Bonanza Page

Friend to the stars, Ruby hasn't let her famous connections go to her huge furry head (. . . well, except that time she dated XXXXX - sorry monSTAR fans we had to blank out the name to protect the star's identity!) As the super roving reporter for *Shrillboard Magazine*, Ruby likes to put a few puzzles on her pages as well as all the gossip, to keep her fans' star-struck brains from totally shrivelling up.

How many squares can you count?

How many building blocks are stacked up here?

Where are the The Worldies?

Fill in the number of times you find each Moshling in the circles below.

All about Dynamite Diavlo!

Handle with care - will burn on contact! These scorching winged fireball monsters are fiery and super sneaky, but underneath all that sizzly-fizzly lava in their cratery heads, there is a happy, fangtastically cheeky critter. Just don't make them angry or you will get a very nasty lava-ery surprise! Yow!

Name: Diavlo

....

My Owner Name: Bracke

....

Owner's Age:

....

My Owner's Language:

....

I'm Feeling:

....

My Owner is Feeling:

....

My Owner's Favourite Shoes:

....

My Favourite Moshling:

....

My Owner's Favourite Moshling:

....

Colour your own hot-head friend and fill in all the details on the Moshi profile card.

Answers

Page 1
Blingo is hidden on page 3; Shambles is hidden on page 9; Gracie is hidden on page 13 and the Hairy Green Paw Chair is hidden on page 7.

Page 2
Master of Moshi Fact or Fib?
1. FACT
2. FIB - he freaks out if he sees one. FYI, Moshi fans, his favourite food is Fairy Cake.
3. FIB - there is one eye on top of the letter 'I'.
4. FIB - they graze in a field at the end of Sludge Street.
5. FACT - Precious Prisms hate smudges, especially on themselves!
6. FACT
7. FIB - he is the biggest monster in Monstro City.
8. FIB - they are Dinos.
9. FIB - his ship is called the Cloudy Cloth Clipper.
10. FACT. Did you know that they come from a lost tribe found deep in the Gombala Gombala Jungle?

Page 3
Roxy's Rockin Rox Picture Patterns
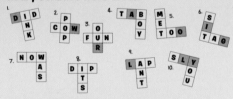

Page 4
Roary Scrawl's Word Cross

Roary Scrawl works on the DAILY GROWL paper.

Page 5
Gilbert Finnster's Word Shuffle Page
1. Gilbert Finnster's shop is called Paws 'n' Claws.
2. The five Moshlings are: OOMPAH, NIPPER, O'REALLY, CHERRY BOMB and TINGALING

Page 6
Buster Bumblechops' Mystery Moshlings

Sooki-Yaki   Jeepers   Mr Snoodle   Ecto   Honey

Page 8
Poshi Moshi or Noti?
1. Yellow, 2. A blue monster eye, 3. Two, 4. Her computer screen
5. Purple, 6. 3 items, 7. 55 Rox, 8. Up and down, 9. Cutie Pie,
10. Orange with yellow polka dots.

Page 9
Cap'n Buck's Flag Frenzy
1. South Africa, 2. Tanzania, 3. Japan, 4. Cameroon, 5. Iceland,
6 Belgium, 7 Argentina, 8. Canada.

Page 10
Tamara Tesla's Maths Mash
1. $0 \times 12 = 0$
2. $77 \div 11 = 7$
3. $102 - 17 = 85$
4. $1 + 2 + 3 + 4 + 5 + 6 = 21$
5. 2 4 8 16 32 64
6. 11 22 33 44 55 66
7. 31, 37, 43, 49, 55, 61, 67, 73, 79, 85
8. Four lumps will cost 168 Rox.
9. You will have to pay 75 Rox.
10. Billy Bob Baitman can make thirteen pairs of boots. He will have one boot left over.
11. Moe Yukky took 195 minutes to clean up his shop.
12. You spend 38 Rox. You have 46 Rox left.

Page 11
Prof. Purplex's Perplexing Puzzles
1. 15, 39, 63, 87, 111, 135
2. 212, 197, 182, 167, 152, 137

Page 12
Tyra Fang's Colourful Crazy Quilts
M is the odd one out.
The pairs are: B/E, J/L, A/I, C/N, D/F, G/O, H/K

Page 13
Ruby Scribblez's Scare Squares and Blocks Bonanza Page
There are 41 squares. There are 105 blocks.

Page 14
Where are the The Worldies?

2 Mini Bens
3 Libertys
1 Cleo
3 Rockys